GROWING

—into your—

SOUL

GROWING

—into your—

SOUL

A Celebration of Jewish Life for Your Bar or Bat Mitzvah

Rabbi Larry Tabick

Hylas Publishing
Irvington, New York

Hylas Publishing

First Published in 2005 by Hylas Publishing
129 Main Street, Irvington, New York 10533

Publisher: Sean Moore
Creative Director: Karen Prince
Art Director: Gus Yoo
Editorial Director: Lori Baird
Designers: Shamona Stokes, Betsy Ho
Editor: Hannah Choi
Picture Editor: Anne-Marie Ehrlich
Book conceived by Lauretta Dives

www.hylaspublishing.com

First American Edition published in 2005
10 9 8 7 6 5 4 3 2 1

ISBN: 1-59258-090-4

Printed and bound in Italy
Distributed by National Book Network

To Jackie, without whom my soul would never have grown.

And thanks to Lauretta & Martin,
Without whom this little book would never have happened.

Table of Contents

Introduction 9

First Verse
Growing into Our Souls 11

Significant Days
of the Year

Shabbat {Sabbath}
Shabbat 14
The Feet of Our Souls 16

Pesach {Passover}
Pesach 19

Shavuot {Feast of Weeks}
To Hear the Voice 20

Tisha Be'av {Fast of the Ninth of Av}
Exile 23

Rosh Hashanah {New Year}
The Warrior to War 24
New Year, New Glasses 26

Yom Kippur {The Day of Atonement}
Al Chet 29

Sukkot {Feast of Tabernacles}
The Sukkah of Peace 30

Simchat Torah {Rejoicing in the Torah}
Simchat Torah 33

Chanukah {The Festival of Lights}
Chanukah Lights 34

Purim {Feast of Lots}
P.U.R.I.M. 37

Momentous Days of our Lives

BIRTH
To Be Born 40
These Parents 42

SCHOOL DAYS
Fizzykx 45

BAR & BAT MITZVAH/CONFIRMATION
A Step along the Path 46

ENGAGEMENT & MARRIAGE
True Love? 49

BECOMING A PARENT
Gifts 50

OLD AGE
When You're Old 53

DEATH AND BEYOND
Great-Auntie 54

Our Heritage: Values and Virtues

LOVE OF GOD
Before Before 58
Infinite Love 60

LOVE OF THE JEWISH PEOPLE
Yehudah/Avraham/Adam 63

LOVE OF ISRAEL
King David's Tomb 64

LOVE OF NEIGHBOR
Mother/Father 67

HONESTY AND TRUTH
Binocular Vision 68

FAITH
Kingdom of Faith 71

TALLIT, TEFILLIN
Light & Might 72

THE SIDDUR
Prayer Book Revision 75

TALMUD TORAH {STUDY OF TORAH}
What Is Torah? 76

PRAYER
In Our Own Way 79

ECOLOGY
Birdsong in November 80

REMEMBERING THE PAST
Second-hand Memories 83
Dweller Intense 85

CHARITY
Saves from Death 86

THE MESSIANIC HOPE
Messiah 89

Final Reflection

Ask Your Soul 91

Glossary 92
Credits 94

Introduction

Bar or Bat Mitzvah is, ultimately, a cosmic event. It may not seem like that, as you and your family get caught up in its loving embrace—the countless, complex preparations before, and the cherished memories afterward—but it is cosmic nevertheless.

Of course, it is a very important event in your life, marking the transition toward taking full adult responsibility for yourself, and, even more significantly, for others. And, of course, it is also a pivotal event in the life of your family, as you begin to move into the world of your parents and wider family and society.

For the Jewish community too, Bar or Bat Mitzvah is important, for the community relies on its future generations, on young people like you, to support it; otherwise it has no future. Hopefully, the process of learning and training that you went through has helped to make you into a knowledgeable, committed adult Jew.

All this is well known, and the chances are your rabbi or Jewish teacher or someone close to you said this at your service or at your party.

Judaism, however, also tries to teach us how to see our lives from a cosmic point of view. It has been said that Judaism follows a spiral version of history. We move forward on a line from Creation, through the Exodus from Egypt and the Revelation of Torah at Mount Sinai, to the Messianic Age in the longed-for future. But we also move in a circular pattern. Each year brings its seasons, and each season its festivals and fasts. Circle and line are not separate, but intertwined, spiralling around a common center. Our festivals and fasts link us to our past, but also to our future, as do our life-cycle events: Brit and Baby-Naming, Bar and Bat Mitzvah, Weddings and Funerals. And in the center is God.

By becoming Bar or Bat Mitzvah, you have linked yourself with the history of our people, and with its journey into the future—a future that leads ultimately to a better world. In order to prepare ourselves for that world, we need to try to be better people. May this book help you in that task.

Mazal tov on your Big Day! May you grow into your soul in the years ahead.

Rabbi Larry Tabick

GROWING INTO OUR SOULS

When we were kids,
Our parents bought us
Clothes
That were too big for us,
Saying,
"You'll grow into them."

We grow into our souls
Like we grew into our clothes.

significant days of the year

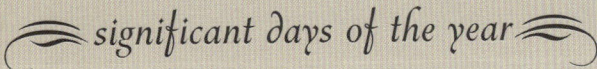

Shabbat {Sabbath}

SHABBAT

Shabbat rest doesn't happen of itself.

Timelessness has to be purchased
within
time.

Eternity emerges from
and
within
time,
Shabbat emerges from
the working days,
like shoots from the soil.

With roots firmly planted, budding flower waiting to grow

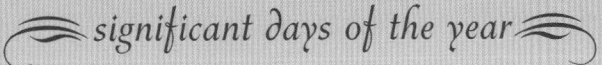

Shabbat {Sabbath}

the FEET *of our* SOULS

Shabbat is
for ritualized, planned laziness.
for virtuous nonproductivity.
for restricted consumerism.

Shabbat is
for idle conversation.
for games of the intellect.
for inspiration, not perspiration.
for composing poems in your head.

Shabbat is
for dancing

on the feet of our souls.

Two dancers, light on their feet

Passover ceremony from the 15th century

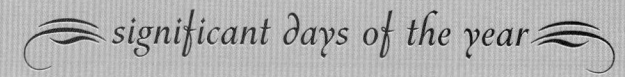

{Passover} # Pesach

PESACH

Political emancipation,
Spiritual liberation,
Revival of vegetation
All come together
In a great symphony of being,
A harmony for the seeing,
A litany of well-being.
So, listen,
Laugh
And be free.

Shavuot {Feast of Weeks}

to HEAR the VOICE

What does it mean to hear the voice of God?
What did we hear
      when we stood at Sinai,
            & received the Ten Sayings
                  on that first Shavuot?

i don't remember, but ...
Some say we heard
      the Ten Sayings.
Some say we heard
      the First Saying:
            "I am the Eternal your God Who brought you up out of
            the land of Egypt ..."
Some say we heard
      the First Word:
            Anochi, "I am."
Some say we heard
      the First Letter:
            a silent '*alef*, an absence of sound.

To hear the voice of God
      is to hear
            the silence that underlies all the noise of the world,
                and to know what is good, beautiful and true.

Moses receives the tablets of law on Mount Sinai

Israelites in chains before Nebuchadnezzar, King of Babylon

{Fast of the Ninth of Av} # Tisha be'Av

EXILE

Exile comes in many forms.

Exile from one's birthplace:
We Jews see this in our history
Feel it in our bones.
i look at you
and see many
who fled persecution
and some who fled
rather than persecute.

Exile from one's family:
Treading a different path
That sets us at odds
With those we love
And who, we hope,
Still love us.

Exile from our past:
Living in denial
Of where we come from,
Of who we were.
Erasing a part of ourselves
That seems not to fit
With what we think
We are now.

Exile from our values:
Driving in
Our decency,
Our love,
Our compassion
In the name of
Security.

Driving in
Our respect for others,
Our self-respect
In the name of
Defense.
Driving them in,
Because we can never
Drive them out.

Exile of the *Shechinah*:
When we cut ourselves off
From the God within
And deny the God within
Others.

Redeem us
From exile!

Rosh Hashanah {New Year}

the
WARRIOR
to WAR

The sound of the Shofar
bizarre
primitive
primal
calling the warrior to war
calling the warrior in me
to war
against
my implacable foe
my nearest and dearest
enemy:
my selfishness;

calling the warrior to war
calling the warrior in me
to war
against
the warrior in me;
calling the warrior in me
to make peace with
the warrior in me.

Pharaoh's army caught in the Red Sea

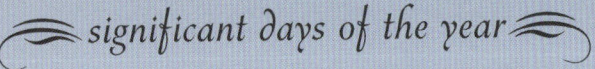
Rosh Hashanah {New Year}

New Year/New Glasses

Rosh Hashanah is like having an eye examination:

Are we seeing the world

and ourselves

in the proper perspective?

Yom Kippur is like getting new glasses,

But will we wear them?

Will we allow ourselves to get used to them

Or let them sit in a drawer

Gathering dust

'Til next year?

Seeing in a new way

עמק אימה

שושן

ש בת שבתון לקיימי
ש ורשיענת סיימי
ש רים יחד לציימי
עתמטי יסוחזתי
ב טהה בחזן מזסרזתי
ב סתקעה תנידזתי
ב כפל להשאין ירזתי
מזה בפעל יצרי
ת ובמת המה היזצרי
ת רזפה התת לעצזרי
ם בל להאפיל ליצרי

Prayer for the morning of the Day of Atonement

Yom Kippur {The Day of Atonement}

AL CHET

Didn't i confess this last year?
    Didn't i do it again this year?

i am caught in a loop:
    i pass through the same sins every year;
    or they pass through me,
    but actually, there is nothing passive here.

i do them year by year
    without end
        only to confess them once more.

It would be so easy to despair
    but ...
        what if there were a loving God?

Then God would know
    how weak i am
        and forgive
            year by year.

29

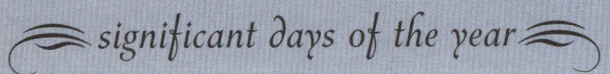

Sukkot {Feast of Tabernacles}

the SUKKAH of PEACE

A sukkah's fragile.
One storm
And it's destroyed
A mass of twisted
Wood
And leaves.

Yet
Each year
We rebuild anew
For the glory of God
Who set us free.

Peace is fragile.
One storm
And it's destroyed
A mass of twisted
Bodies
And souls.

Yet
We must
Rebuild anew
For the glory of God
Who made us all.
"Spread over us the sukkah of Your peace."

The wind blows across the peaceful path

The triumph of a Torah scholar

{Rejoicing in the Torah} # Simchat Torah

SIMCHAT TORAH

Why is this day
such a joy,
for every Jew,
girl or boy?

'Cause Torah is the best
of goods,
the best of goods
in your neighborhood.

Maybe you don't study it
every day.
Maybe other things
get in the way.

No need to
worry!
No need to
feel harried!

You can still dance
at a wedding,
even if you're not
married!

(Yes, i know it's doggerel,
but—hey!— it's
Simchat Torah!)

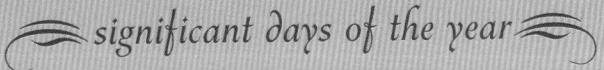
Chanukah {The Festival of Lights}

CHANUKAH LIGHTS

We truly observe Chanukah
    when we know
        that lighting the candles
            means
                revealing the light of the soul;

    when we know
        that true dedication
            means
                nourishing the light of the soul;

    when we know
        that the truest giving
            means
                sharing the light of the soul.

Chanukah lamp from Jerusalem

Coronation of Esther as Jewish Queen of Persia by King Ahasuerus

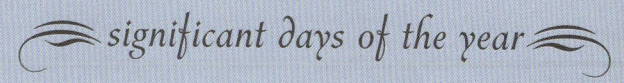

{Feast of Lots} # Purim

P.U.R.I.M.

Purim Uncovers Rarely Innocuous Meanings.
Purim Underlines Really Important Messages.
Purim Undulates Raucous Intentional Mayhem.
Prophecy Underpins Religiously Interpreted Missive.

Pouring Unstinting Rum Inculcates Madness.
Please Understand Risks Involving Minions.
Probably Understating Royalty-Involving Maneuvers.
Purely Undercover Religionists Instill Masses.

Please Undertake Raw Intoxicated Mission.

Give me another drink,
and I'll go on like this for hours.

momentous days of our lives

Birth

to ℬ*e* BORN

What was it like
    to be born?
    to enter the world
        as a new soul?

Our sages say
    our souls came pure
        from God
    and will one day
        return there;
    and every night
        visit there
            in our dreams.

Being born was
    like waking up.

Open your eyes
    and be amazed at all
        the wonder
        the beauty
        the love
            in the world.

The cradle of new life

Birth

these PARENTS

i was born into turmoil
—warring parents,
a clash of cultures,
a cacophony of languages,
competing theologies—
and in the midst of that,
i struggled to find out
who i was.

Why did i pick these parents?

So i could learn to be a better parent?
So i could find beauty in all cultures?
So i could appreciate that all languages are rich in their own terms?
So i could realize that all religions depict Truth in their own unique way?
—while i strive to be me.

Why did you pick your parents?

The family room

The red Pesiod plum, with fruit fly

School Days

FIZZYKX

My high school days

were spent in a daze,

caused by riding the subway each morning

the length of New York City.

Each afternoon

i would ride part way

with my friend John Hayes,

tall, gaunt, funny.

Together we endured

biology class,

counting sleeping drosophila, fruit flies;

chemistry class,

asking our Jewish teacher 'bout the chemistry of *shmutz*;

and on the train,

we would scribble in our note books

as many ways as we could think of to spell "Physics."

i haven't seen him since graduation.

i never kept in touch.

But when i think of him,

in my mind, I am back on the train

trying to spell "Physics"

with f's, z's, k's and x's;

and i'm laughing.

Bar & Bat Mitzvah

a STEP *along the* PATH

Growing up is hard.
Being grown up is harder.
You don't wake up one morning and
"POOF!"
you're grown up.

Growing up is not about age or size:
i know many childish grown-ups,
many grown-up children.

Laws need neat cut-off dates
—old enough to vote,
old enough to marry,
old enough to be responsible—
because laws like things to be neat.

Life isn't always so neat.
But laws can mark a step along the path.

At 13
you can take a step along the path
towards becoming who you really are.
Take that step with care and confidence.

The ascent to Ariccia, Italy

A lovers' walk

Engagement & Marriage

TRUE LOVE?

It must have been your smile
    that first attracted me to you;
        your smile and your shining eyes.
            They made me want to smile, too.

Thirty years, three children,
    and innumerable crises later,
        we're still smiling.

Is that true love,
        or what?

Becoming a Parent

GIFTS (based on *Abraham Maimonides' comments on Genesis 33:5*)

Children are the gifts God gave me.
Gifts i don't deserve.
Souls given into our care
'til they can make their own way.

Grant me the patience
to show them the love they deserve,
the love that comes from You
through us
—the guardians of these,

Your gifts.

Grant me the forbearance
to let them go towards their freedom,
the freedom that comes from You
to them
—the freedom to become
the best they can.

Future US President Franklin D. Roosevelt on his father's shoulder

Frost on the field

Old Age

WHEN YOU'RE OLD

When you're old
(They say)
It is always winter,
When life waits in the wings
For its turn
In the
Great Adventure.

Death and Beyond

GREAT-AUNTIE

Great-auntie, aged 90,
On her niece's death,
Said: "i know it's silly
But i keep thinking:
As she was dying,
Did she know?
And if she's in heaven
Does she know
She's dead?"

Sometimes the silly questions
Hold deep mysteries.

And as she asks,
We both know that soon
Great-auntie will know
The answers.

i sit in stunned silence
Before her courage & wisdom.

The old woman tossed up in a basket

our heritage: values & virtues

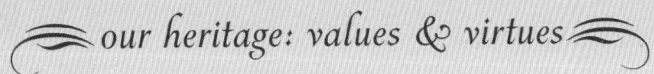

Love of God

BEFORE BEFORE

Before Before
And After,
When there was no world
No stars, no sun,
When there was Nothing and Nowhere,
There was God.
Alone.

And God took hands
That were not hands.
And God formed
That which was not formed.
And God brought forth
That which had never been.
And it was.
And it is.
Light.

And through aeons
Upon aeons
The universe grew
'Til it begot you.

And now,
Follow the light
Back to
Before Before
And After,
Back to Nothing and Nowhere,
And find Me there.
As I was.
As I am.
As I always will be.
"I AM."

Earth rising over Moon's horizon

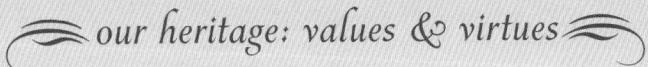

Love of God

INFINITE LOVE

You are infinite love
    in infinite space.
i am/we are infinite love
    in a finite space.
No wonder i/we get
    distracted
        frustrated
            contracted
                prostrated.

Infinite love needs
    to respond to
        infinite love
            that it may overcome
                finite space,
          that i/we may overcome
              distraction
                frustration
                  contraction
                    prostration,
                      that i/we may overcome.

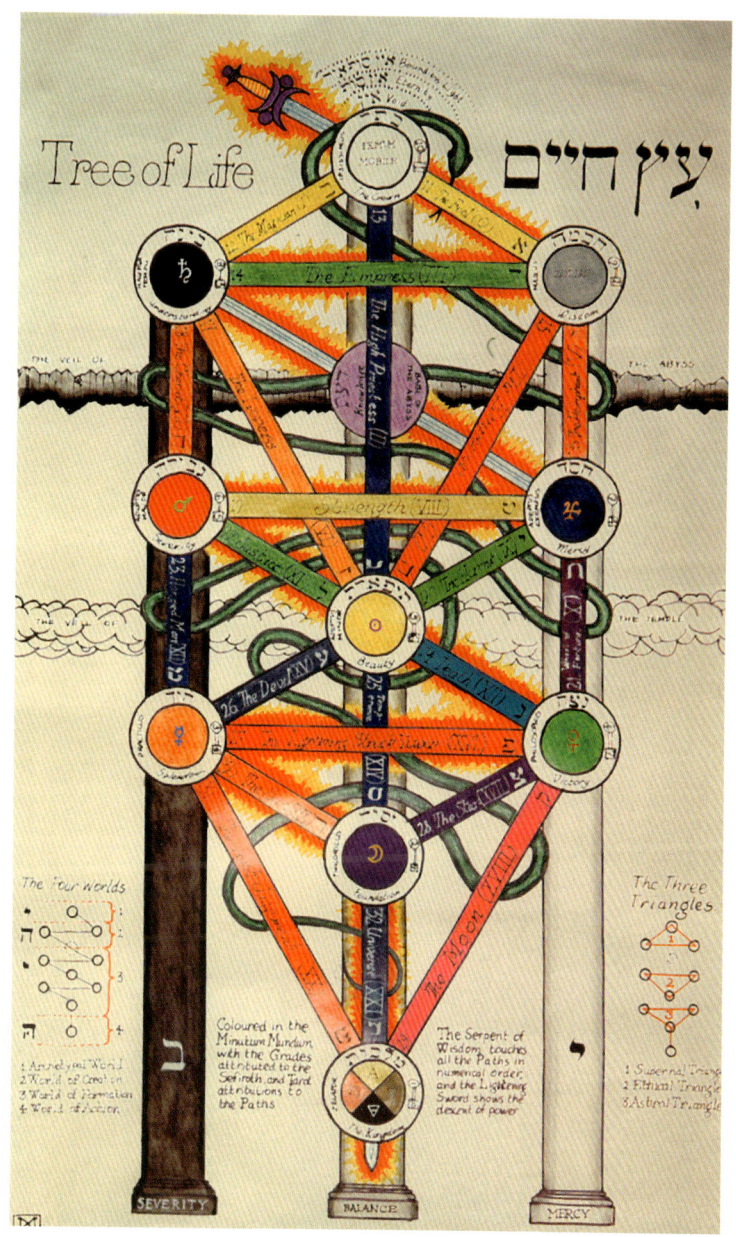

The Tree of Life, with the Ten Sefirot, or divine energies

Adam created by God

Love of the Jewish People

Who am i?
>i start with where i am,
>>with who i am,
>>>and strive to be me.

YEHUDAH

i am Yehudah/Judah,
>flawed ancestor of the Jews,
>acknowledging God in my flawed state.
>>All Jews are my sisters and brothers.

AVRAHAM

i am Avraham/Abraham/Ibrahim,
>ancestor of peoples,
>discoverer of God,
>embodiment of loving kindness.
>>All Christians & Muslims are my sisters and brothers.

ADAM

i am Adam,
>whose name is no name
>but a prayer,
>>a statement of what is
>>and what could be:
>>>Adam: "the person, the human being"
>>>Adam: *ðam* + *alef*, blood + The One.
>>>All people are my sisters and brothers.

Who are you?

63

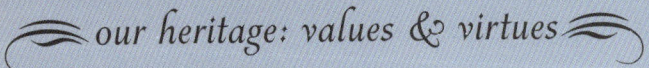

Love of Israel

KING DAVID'S TOMB

Entering the large room
    i stand behind the little fence
    that divides us from the great tomb,
                    just a little beyond our reach.

Is King David really buried here?
    Does it matter?

i take a Bible
    down from an ancient shelf
        and read his most famous work
                —GOD is my shepherd—

and i am awestruck
    in the presence of
        the prayers of millennia.

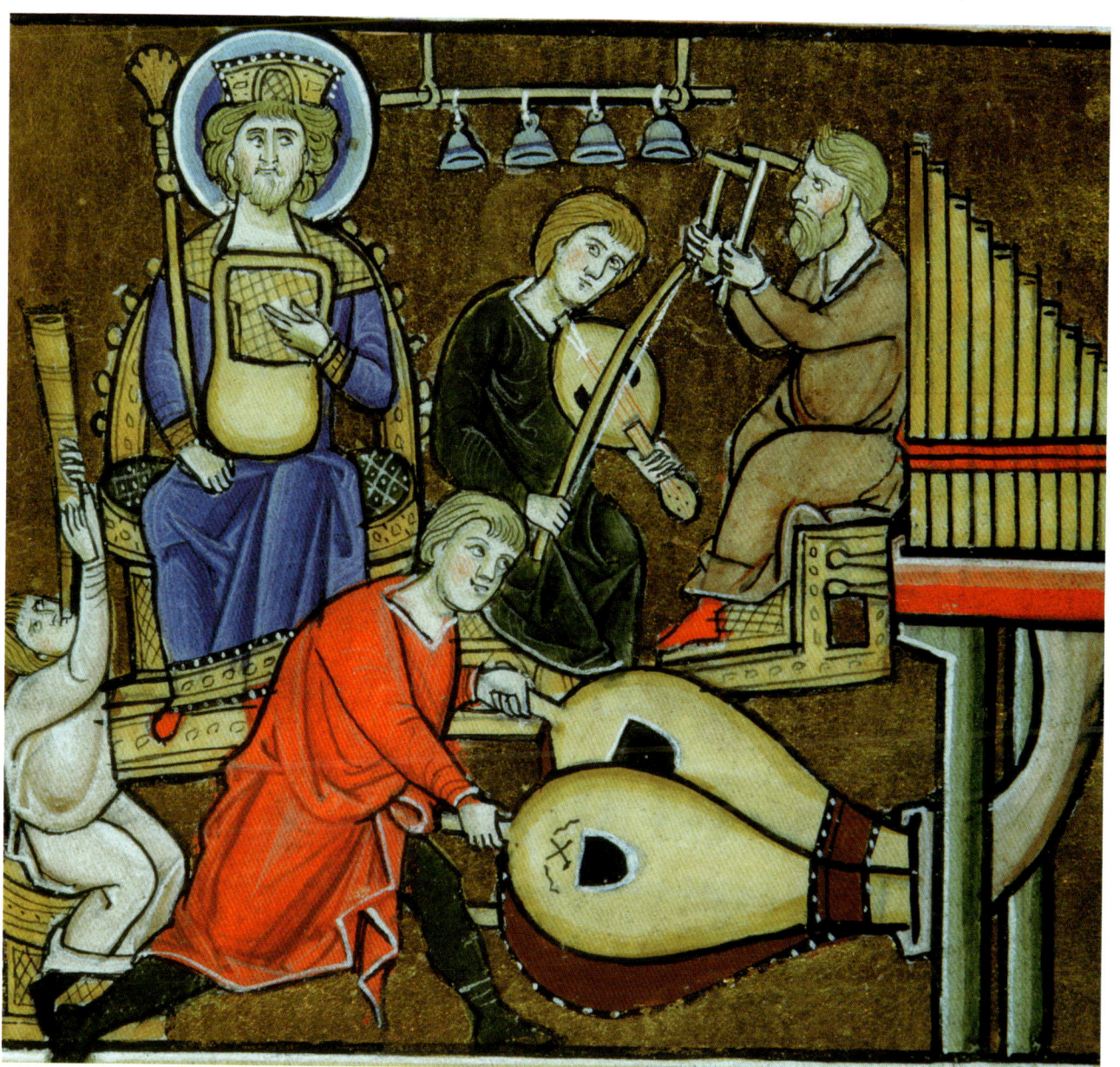

King David with musicians

Hillel's golden rule

Love of Neighbor

MOTHER/FATHER

Divine Mother,
Divine Father,
You are both
To me.

Help me
To see
Your Face
In the face
Of those
i see.

Honesty & Truth

BINOCULAR VISION

My eyes see differently.
Close up
There are two of everything.
Overlapping
But not the same.
If i step back from an object,
The two become one.

God and i see differently.
God judges me,
And i judge myself.
Overlapping
But not the same.
If i step back from my life,
The two may become one.

Camel near the pyramids outside Cairo, Egypt

The Middle East, Persian Gulf, and the Red Sea

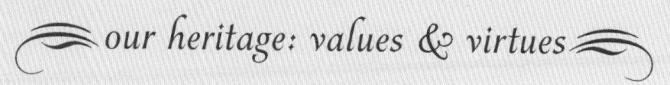

Faith

KINGDOM of FAITH

The autonomous, free Kingdom of Faith
Is a vast country, situated between
The Mountains of Skepticism
And the Sea of Gullibility.
It is bounded on one side by
The dictatorial regime of Fanaticism
And on the other side by
The anarchic desert country of Indifference.
Its terrain and climate are varied,
And though the weather is generally mild,
The warm breeze of Inner Peace
Occasionally gives way to the cold wind of Doubt.
The land is very well sign-posted, yet
Travellers have been known to get lost
And inadvertently stray into foreign territory
With disastrous consequences.
The Sovereign is gracious and beneficent
And its population compassionate.
Visitors are most welcome.
There is plenty to see.
You can wander about, peripatetically,
Looking at the sights,
Or settle in one place to admire the view.
So, be sure to visit;
You may never want to leave.

Tallit, Tefillin

LIGHT & MIGHT

With my *tallit*
    i wrap myself in God's love
                         and light.

With my *tefillin*
    i wrap myself in God's discipline
                         and might.

With love and strength,
    light and might,
        i can begin to pray
            to gather my energies
               for another working day.

The interior of a synagogue

Prayer ceremony from illustrated Hebrew prayer book

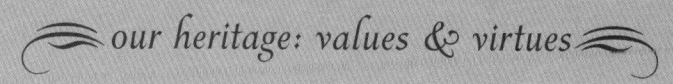
The Siddur

PRAYER BOOK REVISION

Old prayers, new prayers,
Doesn't matter,
Long as they're You-prayers,
Long as they're help-me-to-be-a-good-Jew-prayers.

Old prayers, new prayers,
Doesn't matter,
Long as they're real prayers,
Stop-&-think-&-feel prayers.

Old prayers, new prayers,
Doesn't matter,
Long as they're go-beyond-myself-
And-reach-out-to-You-prayers.

Let them teach me.
Let them reach me.
Let them bring me closer to You-prayers.

Talmud Torah {Study of Torah}

What Is Torah?

What is Torah?,
     i ask.
My teachers say:

    It is the history of our people,
        our past.
    It is the source of our practice,
        our present.
    It is our hope for humanity,
        our future.

       It is the water that refreshes our life;
         the wine that gladdens our heart;
         the milk that gives us nourishment;
         the honey that tastes so sweet;
         the warm bath that cleanses us;
         the mirror in which we see ourselves
            and the world.

When we take Torah into our hearts
        we know that
           God dwells there too.

The Torah displayed to the congregation

A red tabby, purring on the couch

Prayer

IN OUR OWN WAY

We worship God
      each in our own way:

i sit with *tallit* and *tefillin* on
      and say my prayers.

The cat curls up on the couch
      and purrs contentedly.

Maybe i need to learn to purr.

Ecology

BIRDSONG *in* NOVEMBER

Birdsong at midnight
In November.
(Where have all our little birds gone?)
Foxes roaming our streets
Raiding dustbins.
Flowers by the motorway
Covered in the fine dust of diesel fumes.

Life will go on without us,
But crippled,
Limping,
Ailing,
Because we do not revere it,
Or fear it
Enough.
Because we did not mend it,
Or tend it
Enough.

The earth will not forget us.
Our garbage will be here
Long after we are gone.
One day, life will be diverse again.
One day, the trend will reverse again.
Because
Life will go on without us.

We have betrayed life
And now, in desperation,
As we stare into
The Abyss
Of Our Own Making
We turn to its Author
And, with incredible *chutzpah*,
Asking for forgiveness we do not deserve
And for help we could have given ourselves.

The magpie in November

Marc Chagall's "The Rabbi"

Remembering the Past

SECOND-HAND MEMORIES

Chagall's elderly man with *tefillin*,
   my childhood friend,
      always hung on my mother's
         living room wall
            because it reminded her
               of her Zaydeh.
A pious, spiritual man
    who accepted a daughter's Shabbos work
       because she would be helping people in need.
A patient, loving man
    who loved a shrewish, older wife,
       who recognized one daughter for her beauty
         and respected the other for her mind.
A warm-hearted man
    who could bring comfort, love
       and chocolates
         to a troubled granddaughter.
A travelling peddler
    who roamed 'round countries
       old and new
         selling odds and ends
           just to make ends meet.

And a good man
    who deserved a better death
       than the one he got:
         mind gone and body lingering.
And with mom's death that Tuesday
    my last link is gone
       to my ancestor
         dead seven years at my birth
           that i know only
              as her Zaydeh.
Yet now i go and pack
    up "his" picture
       in cardboard tubing
         ready for shipment
           to my home
         where it can remind me of her
          and of him.
And for the moment,
    he will live again
       on my wall
         as *my* Zaydeh.

83

Jacob's ladder from Earth to Heaven

Remembering the Past

DWELLER INTENSE

"Jacob was a dweller in tents,"
A dweller intense.
Desperate to climb the ladder,
Wrestling with God 'til dawn.
Learning along the way
That there is no escaping
From the evil we set in train.
Learning along the way
That there is no eluding
The plan God set in train.
Learning along the way
How to be himself
Without deceit
Without manipulation.
Learning along the way
How to be Israel.

Charity

SAVES from DEATH

"Charity saves from death."

(Talmud, Bava Batra 10a)

Preposterous?

Maybe not.

I used to know a woman
—my mother-in-law—
who promised to go to a charity lunch.

In the morning, she felt awful
but, she said,
"a promise is a promise";
so, off she went.

As lunch wore on,
she felt worse and worse;
she wrote her check and left.

A friend, seeing her state,
drove her home and
stayed with her 'til the doctor came,
and sent her to hospital.

Had she stayed in bed that morning,

she would never have woken up.

The sick woman

The morning sun over the field

The Messianic Hope

Messiah*

O, beloved children,
It will be so nice,
When the Messiah comes.
May he come in a trice.

His eyes will be like
One double sun,
But higher, brighter,
And silver his tongue.

What have we done, children,
For him to prepare?
—The Messiah, the faithful—
Of him we're aware.

Holding a plow,
With a sword in his hand.
His eyes to heaven,
His feet on the land.

—And who, O children,
Brought you that news so fine?
—The Messiah, the faithful—
For whom we have pined

And watchmen maintained
For that special day—
"The Messiah, Messiah,
Is coming today!"

*A translation of the poem "Moshiach"
by the Yiddish writer Yehoash

The TREE *of the* SOUL.

Richard's,
Library,
Nº 9. Cornhill,
London.

ASK YOUR SOUL

Through aeons upon aeons
and countless bodies
your soul has journeyed
to this nexus
of Space-Time.
At a certain level of awareness,
when you "remember"
that you are an ambassador
of the Most High,
ask your soul:
Why this time?
This place?
Why these parents?
These friends?
This social web?
What am i here to learn?
To do?
To teach?
Ask your soul
and the answers will come.

GLOSSARY

ADAM: In Hebrew, meaning "person, individual, human being," but also the name of the first human being.

AL CHET: Hebrew meaning "for the sin." This is the name given to a Yom Kippur prayer that lists sins for which we are atoning. Each line begins with the words "For the sin we have committed before You by ..."

ALEF: The first letter of the Hebrew alphabet, with a numerical value of "one." It is sometimes used to stand for God.

AVRAHAM/ABRAHAM/IBRAHIM: Hebrew, English, and Arabic forms of the same name, the man from whom all three Western religions (Judaism, Christianity, and Islam) spring.

AVRAHAM BEN HARAMBAM (1186–1237): The only son of the great Jewish thinker Maimonides (Rambam), and a scholar in his own right.

CHAGALL, MARC (1887–1985): The most famous Jewish painter of the twentieth century.

CHANUKAH: Dedication, the winter festival that commemorates the victory of the Maccabees over the empire of Antiochus in the second century BC, marked with the lighting of candles for eight nights.

CHUTZPAH: Hebrew and Yiddish for insolence, audacity, or, in other words, "cheek."

DAM: Hebrew word for "blood."

DAVID, KING: The greatest king of ancient Israel—his tomb is said to be in Jerusalem.

PESACH: Passover, the springtime festival that commemorates the departure of the Jewish people from Egyptian slavery. The Seder meal on the first night of two begins the week of Pesach.

PURIM: Lots, the holiday in late winter or early spring that tells how Mordechai and Esther thwarted the plans of the evil Haman to destroy the Jewish people in ancient Persia.

ROSH HASHANAH: The New Year, set in the early autumn, marked with the blowing of the shofar.

SHABBAT: The seventh day of the week, set aside for rest and not working.

SHAVUOT: The Feast of Weeks, seven weeks after Pesach, commemorating the giving of the Torah on Mount Sinai.

SHMUTZ: Yiddish for "dirt."

SHOFAR: The ram's horn blown on Rosh Hashanah.

SHUL: Yiddish, literally meaning "school," but used for synagogues, "houses of study."

SIDDUR: Prayer book.

SIMCHAT TORAH: Rejoicing with the Torah, a happy occasion at the very end of Sukkot when we finish reading the Torah and then immediately begin all over again.

SUKKAH: A temporary shelter in which Jews are meant to live for the week of Sukkot.

SUKKOT: The Feast of Tabernacles or Booths, a week-long festival of joy just after Yom Kippur. The main observances are waving the lulav (palm frond) and dwelling in a sukkah.

TALLIT: Prayer shawl.

TEFILLIN: Phylacteries, small leather boxes containing biblical verses worn on the left arm and head at weekday morning services.

TISHA be'AV: The Ninth Day of the summer month of Av—a fast day on which we remember the destruction of the Temple in Jerusalem and other tragedies of Jewish history.

YEHOASH (1872–1927): Pen name of the Yiddish poet and Bible translator Yehoash Solomon Bloomgarden.

YEHUDAH/JUDAH: Hebrew and English forms of the name of Jacob's fourth son—the ancestor of the tribe of Judah, and from whom the word "Jew" comes.

YOM KIPPUR: The Day of Atonement—a fast day, ten days after Rosh Hashanah.

ZAYDEH: Yiddish for "grandpa."

CREDITS

Title Page
Book of Psalms, from Kennicott Bible,
Spain, 1476
The Bodleian Library, Oxford
(Kennicott 1 folio 352v)

Introduction
Star of David, from Kennicott Bible,
Spain, 1476
The Bodleian Library, Oxford
(Kennicott 1 folio 122r)

Growing into Our Souls
Handy Spandy, Jack-a-dandy, cut-out paper
toy for children
Private Collection

Shabbat
Helleborus niger without flower by
Gherardo Cibo, 1565
British Library

The Feet of Our Souls
Two dancers, watercolour by Paul Sandby,
1725-1809
Victoria and Albert Museum, London

Pesach
Passover ceremony, 15th century manuscript
Bibliothèque de l'Arsenal, Paris

To Hear the Voice
Moses receives the tablets of the law,
Moutier-Grandval Bible, 8-900 AD
British Library, London

Exile
Hebrews or Israelites in chains before
Nebuchadnezzar, Beatae Elisabeth Psalter,
13th century
Archaeological Museum, Cividale, Friuli

The Warrior to War
The Israelites crossing the Red Sea,
Beatae Elisabeth Psalter, 13th century
Archaeological Museum, Cividale, Friuli

New Year, New Glasses
Victorian mask by Raphael Tuck, c.1900
Mme. Tussauds/Leksak Museum

Al Chet
Morning of the Day of Atonement, Hebrew
prayer book, Germany, c.1320–35
The Bodleian Library, Oxford
(Mich 619 folio 201r)

The Sukkah of Peace
After the Storm, by Carlo Prada, 1884–1960
Galleria d'Arte Moderna Rome

Simchat Torah
Successful student of the Torah being
conducted home, 1/23 engraving by
Bernard Picart, 1673–1733
Galerie Saphir Paris

Chanukah Lights
Chanukah lamp, 1930, from Jerusalem
Private Collection

P.U.R.I.M.
Coronation of Esther as Jewish Queen of
Persia by King Ahasuerus by Vincenzo
Morani, 1813–70
Galeria d'Arte Moderna, Rome

To Be Born
The cradle, 1872 by Berthe Morisot, 1841–95
Musée d'Orsay, Paris

These Parents
Family at a meal, 19th century, France
Private Collection

Fizzykx
The Red Pesiod plum, with fruit fly, from
Tradescant's Orchard, an early 17th century
English manuscript
The Bodleian Library, Oxford
(Ashmole 1461 folio 69)

A Step Along the Path
The Ascent to Ariccia Italy by
Gian Battista Bassi, 1754–1852
Galleria d'Arte Moderna, Rome

True Love
Lovers walking by Giuseppe Pellizza da
Volpedo, 1868–1907
Museo Civico Ascoli Piceno

Gifts
Franklin Delano Roosevelt, 1882–1945, 32nd
President of the United States of America
(1933–1945) eighteen months old, with his
father James Roosevelt, 1934–5
Culver Pictures

When You're Old
Hoarfrost, 1873 by Camille Pissarro,
1830–1903
Musée d'Orsay Paris

Great Auntie
The old woman who was tossed up in
basket by Aliquis, 1884
The Bodleian Library, Oxford

Before Before
View of Earth rising above Moon's horizon
from Apollo II, July 1969, from NASA

Infinite Love
Tree of Life showing the ten spheres by
Mark Penney Maddocks
Private Collection

Yehudah/Avraham/Adam
Adam created by God, Visions of Saint
Hildegard of Bingen, Book of the Works of
God, Latin Codex, 12th century
Biblioteca Civica, Lucca

King David's Tomb
King David with musicians,
Beatae Elisabeth Psalter, 13th century
Archaeological Museum, Cividale, Friuli

Mother/Father
Jewish teacher and pupil learning
Hillel's golden rule: "What is hateful to
you, do not do to another."
The Coburg Pentateuch c.1395
British Library

Binocular Vision
Camel near the pyramids outside Cairo,
Egypt. Stereoscopic photograph c.1920
Private Collection

Kingdom of Faith
Middle East, Persian Gulf, and the Red Sea,
from Catalan Mappamundi, 1502,
by Alberto Cantino
Biblioteca Estense Modena

Light & Might
Interior of Synagogue by K. J. Polak
Israel Museum, Jerusalem

Prayer Book Revision
Prayer ceremony from illustrated Hebrew
prayer book, Germany, 1471.
The Bodleian Library, Oxford
(Opp 776 folio 20v)

What is Torah?
The Torah is displayed to the congregation
1723 engraving by Bernard Picart, 1673–1733
Galerie Saphir, Paris

In Our Own Way
Red Tabby, lithograph by Sheila Roberts,
1971
Private Collection

Birdsong in November
The magpie by Claude Monet, 1840–1926
Musée d'Orsay, Paris

Second-hand Memories
The Rabbi by Marc Chagall, 1887–1985
The Galleria d'Arte Moderna, Venice,
Copyright ARS 2004

Dweller Intense
Jacob's ladder, illustration by C. M. Foy in
L'Histoire Sainte, France, 1948
Private Collection

Saves from Death
The sick woman by Pietro Longhi, 1702–85
Ca Rezzonico Museum, Venice

Messiah
The countryside near Dresda, Norway by
Johan Christian Clausen Dahl, 1788–1857
Bergen Art Gallery

Ask Your Soul
Tree of the Soul by Jacob Boehme, 1575–1624
Private Collection

תַּם וְנִשְׁלַם

תּוֹדָה לְאֵל עוֹלָם.

Finished and done,
Thanks to the One.